Johannesburg

in 3 Days:

**The Definitive Tourist Guide Book That
Helps You Travel Smart and Save Time**

Book Description

Johannesburg is not a prime travel destination, but it is drawing more visitors, thanks to its thought-provoking museums and attractions and a regeneration program in the city. We'll show you the highlights of this unique city, and the top places to see and experience.

Included:

- How to get to Johannesburg
- How to get around easily once you arrive
- Where to find a luxury, midrange or cheap hotel
- Where to eat, for all kinds of tastes
- The highlights you won't want to miss
- Festivals and special events that may be taking place while you're there

Packed with information and advice, this concise guide will assist you in getting the most from a three-day trip to Johannesburg.

The People of Johannesburg

As of 2014, Johannesburg had a population of over four million people. It is generally referred to as the most densely populated and largest city found in South Africa. 75% of the population are African, with whites accounting for 16% and colored for 6%. 4% of Johannesburg residents are Indian.

In addition to treating old customs with respect, the people of Johannesburg love sports, and can often be seen watching cricket or soccer matches, when they're not working. The people who call Johannesburg home, along with tourists, enjoy exploring the many museums and galleries in town. They don't slow down at night, either – Joburg, as it's often called, has a simply amazing nightlife.

Language

South Africa has 11 official languages, and all are spoken in various parts of Johannesburg. The languages most often used are Afrikaans and English, and English is understood in most areas. Afrikaans as a language is similar to Flemish and Dutch.

Holidays

** These months see the holidays fall on different dates each year

January 1	New Year's Day
January**	Public Holiday
March 21	Human Rights Day
April**	Good Friday
April**	Family Day
April 27	Freedom Day
May 1	Workers Day
June 16	Youth Day
August 9	National Women's Day
September 24	Heritage Day
September 25	Public Holiday
December 16	Day of Reconciliation
December 25	Christmas Day
December 26	Day of Goodwill

Religious Beliefs

The constitution of South Africa guarantees that people have the freedom to practice the religion of their choice. There are many religions represented in the regional and ethnic diversity, and Christianity is the most often practiced.

South African Christian Denominations

The Christian denominations found in South Africa and in Johannesburg include:

- Anglican & Catholic
- South African Interchurch
- AIC and Holiness
- Protestantism
- Reformed
- Pentecostal

Christians account for nearly 80% of the South African population. There isn't a single dominant denomination, though. The Catholic Church along with Africa-initiated churches, Pentecostal churches and mainstream Protestant churches all have many adherents.

Hinduism in South Africa

People in various provinces in South Africa practice Hinduism, but the total is only a bit over one percent.

Islam in South Africa

Muslims in SA are in the minority, with less than 1.5% of the population estimated to practice Islam.

Judaism in South Africa

The British Empire's rule in South Africa was the time of Jews' first history in South Africa. European settlements were common in the 19th century. Most Jews settled in SA between the 17th and 19th centuries.

Bahá'í Faith in South Africa

The Bahá'í Faith within SA started with 1911 Bahá'í meetings in South Africa. Practitioners of the faith were oppressed during Apartheid. South Africa and the homelands were reunited in 1995 and they formed the Bahá'í National Spiritual Assembly of South Africa. There were an estimated 240,000 adherents to the faith in 2005.

Here is a quick preview of what you will learn in this tourist guide:

- Helpful information about Johannesburg
- Flying into the city
- Transportation tips in town
- Why Johannesburg is such a vibrant tourist spot and what you will find most remarkable about it
- Information on luxury and budget accommodations and what you'll get for your money

- The currency used in Johannesburg
- Tourist attractions you should make time to see
- Other attractions for entertainment and culture
- Events that may be running during your stay
- Tips on the best places to eat & drink for all price points, whether you want simple fare, worldwide dishes or African flavor

Table of Contents

1. Introduction

Johannesburg is also called Joburg, Jozi and eGoli, and it's the largest South African city. It is the capital of the province of Gauteng, the wealthiest province in the country. Johannesburg isn't among the capital cities of South Africa, but it does serve as the seat for the Constitutional Court.

The city proper has over four million people, but if you include the surrounding metropolitan area, it brings the total population to over seven million. It covers a relatively large land area of over 600 square miles.

After gold was discovered in 1886 in the area (which was a farm then), the city was established. Gold is linked to the wealth of the city and the province.

Soweto has been a part of Johannesburg, since the 1990's. The name comes from a simple acronym that meant "South-Western Townships". It started out as a group of settlements just outside Johannesburg, mainly populated by gold mine workers of native African origin. During apartheid, blacks had to live in Soweto. They were not allowed to have a residence in the city of Johannesburg itself.

A Brief History of Johannesburg

Groups of people who spoke Bantu began moving into South Africa in the 13th century. Most people at the time were farmers, or mined and smelted common metals from the area.

Many small mining and related towns were destroyed during the wars of the 18th and 19th centuries that emanated from Zululand. The native people were driven away.

In 1884, miners discovered the Witwatersrand gold reef. This started a gold rush, and the true city of Johannesburg, which was named in 1886.

Gold attracted many people to the area, so organization was necessary. Within 10 years, the population of Johannesburg would grow to 100,000.

White miners from every continent populated the new town. In addition, there were native tribesmen who performed unskilled mine work and many native women who brewed beer and cooked for the migrant workers.

The city also included many European gangsters and prostitutes, tradesmen, poor Afrikaners, and Zulu men. As the land continued to increase in value, it caused tension between the British and the Boer government of Pretoria. This culminated in the Jameson Raid, ending in 1896.

During this war, many native mine workers left the city, and this created a shortage of laborers. The mine owners brought in workers from China. After the war, black workers would replace them, but many of these Chinese stayed in the city, creating the Chinese community of Johannesburg. During apartheid, these Chinese were classified as "colored", not "Asian". In 1904 the population of the city was over 155,000. Of these, over 83,000 were white.

After the era of apartheid, present-day Johannesburg would be created from eleven pre-existing local authorities. Seven were white and four were colored. The white authorities were subsidized at 90% by taxes, while the black authorities only received 10% from taxes.

In the municipal elections of 2016, the African National Congress, which was the party in power, lost the majority in the city for the first time since they took power in 1994. They received only a bit over 44% of the city vote. The Democratic Alliance and Economic Freedom Fighters agreed to cast their votes for Herman Mashaba, the DA's candidate for mayor. He became the first DA mayor of the city in August 2016.

Neighborhoods

Johannesburg is just one part of a much larger region. It is linked with satellite towns. Sandton and Randburg are in the northern area.

The Central Business District, known as CBD, covers about two square miles of densely packed skyscrapers, including Southern Life Centre, Ponte City Apartments, the Trust Bank Building, Marble Towers and Carlton Centre.

The center of Joburg still retains a grid pattern first used in 1886. The streets are quite narrow, and the area is full of skyscrapers that were constructed in the mid and late 1900s. During that time period, new architectural structures and styles were introduced. Two examples of this style are the Supreme Court Building and the Johannesburg Art Gallery. They were structure of the Beaux Arts style, placed by the British Empire, who was the colonial parent at that time.

South Africa has also been inspired by American architecture, with similarities to this style in buildings like the Corner House and the ESKOM Building. They were designed to emulate the architectural prowess of the United States' New York City.

The suburbs of Johannesburg resulted from urban sprawl. They are regionalized by east, west, north and south, and each has its own personality. While people used to live in the CBD, more people now live in the suburbs.

The greater Johannesburg area has over 500 suburbs covering over 200 square miles. Even though you will see black Africans in all areas of Johannesburg, the greater Johannesburg area is still very racially segregated.

What does Johannesburg offer its Visitors?

Johannesburg wasn't traditionally a prime tourist destination, but many people used it as a transit point for flights to Kruger National Park, Cape Town and Durban. Several attractions have been developed, since people are passing through the city on their way to other destinations.

Recent additions include historical museums, like the Apartheid Museum and Constitution Hill. The Mandela Museum in Soweto is a popular place to visit. It is found in Nelson Mandela's former home.

You can get a great feel for the city's layout if you visit Carlton Centre, in the CBD. Their 50th floor observation deck offers vast vistas of the city and its surrounding area.

For cultural aficionados, Joburg contains art museums and theaters. For lovers of street life, the suburbs of Greenside, Rosebank, Norwood,

Parkhurst, Newton and Melville offer many bars and restaurants.

Shopping is quite often a popular way to spend time while visiting Johannesburg. The city offers upmarket malls, as well as flea markets and African art markets.

2. Key Information about Johannesburg

Money Matters

There is good news for you if you'll be traveling to Johannesburg, even for just a few days. The hotels, attractions and meals are relatively inexpensive.

The rand is the South African currency. It fluctuates dramatically against the U.S. Dollar. One rand is equal to 100 (African) cents. Any amount below 10 cents (African) is virtually worthless.

Bank notes in South Africa are in denominations of R10, R20, R50, R100 and R200. The coins range from 1c (cent) and on to 2c, 5c, 10c, 20c, 50c, R1, R2 and R5. You can exchange cash for rands at foreign exchange bureaus or banks. You may need to prove your physical address for these transactions.

Tipping

It's customary to leave R50 per day per person for hotel housekeeping services. Porters are usually tipped R15 if you have just one or two bags. You can tip the people directly or pay tips at the front desk. If the concierge makes special arrangements for you or reservations at restaurants, etc., you may tip him as well.

Restaurant Tipping

Tipping at restaurants is mainly practiced in larger cities like Johannesburg, and is usually no more than 10% of the total of the bill. If you're in a party of six or more, a service charge of 10% will usually be added to your bill.

3. Transport to and in Johannesburg

Getting to Johannesburg by Plane

O.R. Tambo International Airport is the principal airport serving Johannesburg, whether you're flying in on an international or domestic flight. It is generally regarded as the continent's busiest airport, handling nearly 13 million passengers a year.

Several smaller airports near Johannesburg serve flights to Cape Town and nearby cities, and some are used mainly for small, private aircraft.

Getting to Johannesburg from the Airport

Johannesburg's international airport is 14 miles from the center of the city. You can travel to and from the airport by taxi, train, bus or rental car.

Buses

Public transportation by bus from the airport is available outside the domestic and international terminals. There are city buses and minibuses.

The Rea Vaya, a rapid transit bus, provides affordable, safe and secure public transportation. It travels via dedicated bus lanes and stops every 500 meters.

Taxis

If you aren't familiar with the southern region of Africa, you may not want to use public transportation in Johannesburg unless a local helps to show you where you'll need to debark the bus.

Taxis are usually better options, so you know you'll be dropped at your destination. Metered taxis have yellow "taxi" lights on the roof. They park outside the airport's arrivals area. The trip to the center of town from the airport usually takes about 30-45 minutes.

Trains

The new rail links travel not only to the downtown area from the airport, but also to the suburbs in Pretoria and Sandton. The train station has bus connections and parking, too. The station is on the upper level of the airport between the A and B terminals. There are signs that show you the way.

Johannesburg Rental Cars

You'll see familiar names in the car rental area, including National, Hertz, Budget and Avis, as well as some African rental companies. You can get a good deal by comparing prices. They have sub-compacts, compacts, mid-size and full-size cars available. You can rent luxury cars, too.

Johannesburg Cabs

There are two types of taxis in Joburg – minibus taxis and metered taxis. Metered taxis can't be driven around looking for fares. Rather, the drivers must wait until someone calls them to be picked up. A new program has been implemented by the Gauteng Provincial Government, to try to increase usage of metered taxis.

Payment and Tipping for Taxi's

Taxis are a bit pricey in Johannesburg, but handy to use, since you won't be sitting around while a train or bus goes through stops on the way to your destination. You'll need to call ahead for a taxi.

If you happen to end up with an unmetered taxi, arrange the price before you allow the driver to take off.

These taxi companies run their cars on meters:

Zebra Cabs

Quick Cab

Orange Taxis

Tipping in Taxis

Taxi drivers will be happy to take you to your destination. Minivan taxi drivers don't require tips, but metered car drivers are usually tipped, unless they drive unsafely. Round up to the nearest R10 for in-town driving. If you leave the city by taxi, an acceptable tip is R20. Most taxi drivers work full 24-hour shifts, and if you stop at a gas station, they'll be happy if you'd buy them a juice or soda.

Uber in Joburg

A smartphone and Wi-Fi or a data plan will get you the services of Uber. You've likely used them at home or elsewhere in your travels. Uber has been in use in Joburg since 2014, and their prices are very competitive. You usually won't need to wait more than about five minutes for an Uber car, and if you're in an entertainment or shopping area, you'll have an even shorter wait time.

Public Transport in Johannesburg

Buses

The bus fleet in Johannesburg is operated by a company called Metrobus. It is part of the city. The fleet includes 550 buses and 84 routes. There are also private operators of buses, although they mainly serve the inter-city area.

The main terminal for buses is in Gandhi Square. You can also get more information about the Metrobus service at their customer information walk-in desk.

Passes & Tickets

You'll save money using prepaid tags, as compared to paying cash. There are various colored Metrobus tags that look like phone cards. You can buy them at Computicket outlets.

Johannesburg Trains

The Gauteng Metrorail train system connects the center of Johannesburg to Pretoria, Soweto and many satellite towns in the area. In the southern part of the city, it only serves the older areas. Northern areas, which include Rosebank, Randburg, Midrand and Sandton, are now served by Gautrain's rapid rail link.

4. Accommodations

Luxury Hotels in Johannesburg

If you're accustomed to staying in luxury hotels, you won't be disappointed in Johannesburg. You will usually receive the services you've come to expect in hotels of this type, including restaurants in-hotel, indoor and/or outdoor pool, full service spas, fitness centers, valet parking, 24-hour front desk and airport shuttles.

Prices for luxury hotels are $250-$500 USD and up per night

Saxon Hotel, Villas & Spa
- Close to Hyde Park Corner, Sandton City Mall, Sandton Convention Centre and the Dunkeld West Shopping Centre

Raphael Penthouse Suites

- Close to Nelson Mandela Square, the Johannesburg Stock Exchange, Sandton Convention Centre and Sandton City Mall

Four Seasons Hotel - The Westcliff, Johannesburg

- Close to the Johannesburg Zoo, the South African Museum of Military History, Museum Africa and the University of Johannesburg

InterContinental Johannesburg O.R Tambo Airport

- Close to the International Terminal Duty Free Mall, Bedford Centre Shopping Mall, Kempton Park Golf Club, Festival Mall and Value Mall

Ten Bompas

- Close to the South African Museum of Military History, Sandton City Mall, Dunkeld West Shopping Centre, Hyde Park Corner and Maboneng Precinct

African Rock Hotel

- Close to the Festival Mall, Kempton Park Golf Club and Greenstone Shopping Centre

The Michelangelo Towers

- Close to the Sandton Convention Centre, Sandton City Mall, Johannesburg Stock Exchange and Nelson Mandela Square

Prices for Mid-Range Hotels run $150-$245 USD and up per night

The Residence Boutique Hotel
- Close to the South African Museum of Military History, Johannesburg Zoo, the Victory Theater and the Rosebank Mall

African Pride Melrose Arch Hotel
- Close to Sandton City Mall, Sandton Convention Centre, Wanderers Stadium and the Wanderers Golf Club

10 2nd Avenue Houghton Estate
- Close to the South African Museum of Military History, Johannesburg Zoo, Victory Theater and Constitution Hill

Sandton Sun
- Close to Sandton City Mall, Sandton Convention Centre, Johannesburg Stock Exchange and Nelson Mandela Square

Peermont D'oreale Grande at Emperors Palace

- Close to International Terminal Duty Free Mall, Value Mall, East Rand Mall, K90 Shopping Centre and Kempton Park Golf Club

Davinci Hotel and Suites on Nelson Mandela Square

- Close to Sandton City Mall, Sandton Convention Centre, Johannesburg Stock Exchange and Nelson Mandela Square

Prices for Inexpensive Hotels are $140 USD per night and less

African Pride Irene Country Lodge

- Close to Centurion Golf Estate, Reitvlei Nature Reserve, Smuts House Museum, Jan Smuts Museum and SuperSport Park

Over the Moon Guesthouse

- Close to Cresta Shopping Centre, Johannesburg Botanical Garden, Emmarentia Dam and Randpark Golf Club

Tladi Lodge

- Close to Johannesburg Stock Exchange, Sandton Convention Centre, Sandton City Mall and Nelson Mandela Square

Hyde Park Villas

- Close to Sandton City Mall, Sandton Convention Centre, Johannesburg Stock Exchange, the Wanderers Golf Club and Wanderers Stadium

St Andrews Signature Hotel & Spa

- Close to Bedford Centre Shopping Mall, Glendower Golf Club, Eastgate Shopping Centre and Bruma Lake Flea Market

AshDown House

- Close to Montecasino, Johannesburg Stock Exchange, Sandton Convention Centre, Sandton City Mall and Croc City

The Capital 20 West

- Close to the Johannesburg Stock Exchange, Sandton Convention Centre, Sandton City Mall and Nelson Mandela Square

Airbnb's

For $29 USD a night, you can stay in a beach themed modern bedroom that hopefully will give you a beach-type feel that is lacking within the city. This room includes its own private bathroom and a king size bed, along with a tea and coffee making facility and daily cleaning.

For $239 USD per night, you can stay in an apartment close to OR Tambo International Airport, Rosebank Mall, Sandton City and Montecasino.

If you really want to splurge, $598 USD per night can get you a private house atop a hill, and with breathtaking views. It's surrounded by indigenous trees, gardens, and natural bush. It's an excellent backdrop and setting for your ideal country retreat.

There are more than 300 houses, apartments and condos in the Johannesburg area on the Airbnb site.

Sightseeing

Johannesburg is affectionately referred to as E'Goli, Joburg and Jozi. The city is in the process of evolution from an unsafe stopover to a new and vibrant hub for culture and the arts.

The new galleries, along with art studios, restaurants and cafes, are among the top attractions in the city. Some of the more moving attractions include Constitution Hill and the Apartheid Museum.

The Apartheid Museum

There is arguably no more poignant location in Johannesburg than the Apartheid Museum. Open since 2001, it deals with the 20th century in South Africa. Naturally, apartheid is an integral part of this time in history. This museum shows travelers the rise and fall of the movement of apartheid.

Exhibits in the museum were organized and assembled by designers, historians, film-makers and curators. They include artifacts, text panels, provocative photographs and film footage that illustrate the human stories and events that are part of apartheid.

This museum has been heralded as a beacon of hope, that shows the world the ways in which South Africans are coming to grips with their oppressive past and working towards a joint future that can be called their own by all people of South Africa.

Constitution Hill

This is a living museum telling the story of democracy in South Africa. It is a former military fort and prison that can truly bear testament to the turbulent past of South Africa. It is also home to the Constitutional Court of the country, and this body endorses all citizens' rights.

There is likely no other incarceration site in the country that imprisoned as many world-renowned women and men as those held in the Old Fort, Number Four and the Women's Jail. They include Nelson Mandela, Winnie Mandela, Mahatma Gandhi, Fatima Meer, Albertina Sisulu and Joe Slovo. All of these people served time in this site.

This precinct confined ordinary people by the tens of thousands – women and men of all political agendas, ages, creeds and races. From the elite to the everyman and the immigrant to the indigenous, the history of everyone in South Africa lives within these walls.

Cradle of Humankind

Beneath the rocky outcroppings and rolling grasslands of the Highveld is a limestone cave subterranean network known as the Cradle of Humankind. It is located about 31 miles outside the city of Johannesburg.

Beneath the ground, like ancient buried treasure, are the fossilized remains of ancient plants, animals and humanoids, scattered in the caverns. They provide a rich record of fossils for studies in human evolution.

The Cradle is a UNESCO World Heritage Site. The hominin fossil deposits are so rich that they lend credence to the theory that all humans are descended from a small group of ancestors in Africa.

Carlton Centre

This is a shopping center and skyscraper in downtown Johannesburg. It is 732 feet high, and thus the tallest office building in Africa. It has 50 floors and houses shops and offices. Almost half of the floors are found below ground. Carlton Center links to the Carlton Hotel via a shopping center below-ground, including more than 175 shops.

Hector Pieterson Memorial

This museum commemorates the role of Soweto students in the uprising against apartheid in 1976. It was named for a 12-year old boy who was among the first victims. Many students were shot by apartheid police while they protested the sub-standard education in South Africa's black schools.

The exhibits in the memorial offer background as to why the protests occurred, and illustrate what happened afterward. The museum commemorates the people who died in these uprisings, while celebrating the role of students in the freedom struggle. The memorial and monument are among South Africa's top tourist attractions.

5. Eat & Drink

Restaurants in Johannesburg are well-hosted and the staff are quite attentive. There are multi-culture communities, so there are different tastes to try. There is also a desire for artisanal foods in South Africa, so their dining scene includes local produce, too.

We have broken our restaurant list into three categories, by price. These prices are averages.

Fine dining restaurants: $80 - $315 USD and up for two

Mid-Range restaurants: $50-$80 USD for two

Cheap eats: $11 and less USD for two

Fine Dining Restaurants

View Restaurant at Four Seasons Hotel, The Westcliff - $161 USD for two

This fine dining restaurant is well reviewed by most guests. Their seafood specialties include monkfish & seaweed, lesotho highland trout and fresh kingklip & black beans. They also serve fine meat dishes, like karoo lamb, chicken & lemon, crispy pork belly and prime rib.

Luke Dale Roberts at the Saxon – $307 USD for two

The staff is very attentive here, according to many diners. There are so many choices on the menu at Luke Dale Roberts, too. Among the favorites are crab and grapefruit dressing, apple, daikon and radishes. The popcorn langoustine and miso crumb is popular, as is the seabass tartar with lovage pesto. If you like lamb, try the lamb scotatti, which is smoked lamb with seeds and spices.

The Cube Tasting Kitchen - $118 USD for two

The Cube is known for its creative plating, as well as top notch service and a broad combination of tasty ingredients. The Sunday roast includes fresh flavors of summer, and the popular Thai-inspired Hot & Sour dish includes prawns, tofu, lemongrass and coconut.

Marble −$84 USD for two

Marble is a restaurant on a rooftop, and the views are splendid. The service is exceptional. Among the favorite dishes are the tune ceviche tacos, rib eye and sirloin steaks. For dessert, try the brandy snap ice cream sandwich and the passion fruit and coconut ice cream.

Mid-Range Restaurants - $40 USD to $80 USD

Yamato – $77 USD for two

Yamato serves Authentic Japanese dishes. The Sushi is excellent, as you would expect. The kimchi and crab stick salad are popular, as are the ten don, and the rice and noodle dishes. They also offer gyoza of pork and korokke of beef, and miso cha-shu ramen. Travelers recommend a visit to this restaurant while you're in Johannesburg.

Flames Restaurant at Four Seasons Hotel – $46 USD for two

The Flames Restaurant is tucked up high into the Four Seasons Hotel. The views are breathtaking in the glass lift on the way to dinner. Some of their favorite dishes are the grilled light, fluffy kingklip with toasted almonds and avocado and egg based burger. Their meals offer the perfect blend of texture, salt and spice.

The Fishmonger – $50 USD for two

It's no surprise that the best dishes here are fish. Try the Cajun dry grilled kingklip with sweet potato and steamed spinach. If you're into salads, they have a tasty and filling green salad with lettuce, Parmesan, avo, green peppers and duccah. If you're not watching calories, diners recommend the grilled halloumi at the beginning of your meal or the Italian Kiss at the end.

Café del Sol Classico – $42 USD for two

They have a wide variety of dishes at the Classico. Some of the more popular plates include rack of lamb with pea risotto, the Amatrrociana smoky bacon and gnocchi and ravioli with pastella prawns. For dessert, try the vanilla gelato. All the meals are beautifully plated and offer amazing taste.

Cheap Eats - $30 USD or less

Thava - $27 USD for two

Thava specializes in Indian cuisine. Start with their calamari chili, which includes fried calamari rings with red, green and yellow peppers, soy sauce and vinegar. The chicken and lamb samosas are very popular. Main dish favorites include chicken korma with cream sauce and cashews, and tandoori lamb chops or fish tikka.

Jamie's Italian - $30 USD for two

The feel of this restaurant is part of the pleasing experience. Jamie's has a good selection of champagne and wine. Among their favorite dishes is the crispy calamari with prawn pasta and nachos. They have wonderful desserts too, like the lemon meringue cheesecake and brownies.

Mo-Zam-Bik – $25 USD for two

This restaurant features a variety of interesting dishes. They include Zambeziana poultry with chili, coconut milk and lime. Arroz de coco is their tasty coconut rice. The calamari and chicken with coconut rice and fries is quite tasty. For a starter, try the prawn rissoles, and add ice cream and chocolate rissoles for dessert, if you saved room.

Lucky Bean - $15 USD for two

You can't leave Johannesburg without trying some genuine African food. Lucky Bean is a comfortable restaurant with multiple eating spaces, so it's relatively quiet and quite comfortable. They have attentive servers, too. Among the fine presentation of South African dishes are the fresh ostrich, shredded duck, springbok pie and pork belly.

6. Culture and Entertainment

Johannesburg is South Africa's cultural hub. It features many cultural venues, which makes it a prominent city for cultural and creative industries. The South African Ballet Theatre, Witwatersrand's School of the Arts and the National School of Arts are all located here. So are many libraries, galleries, theatres and museums.

Johannesburg Botanical Garden

This botanical garden is one of the green, vital lungs of Johannesburg. It provides oxygen and digests carbon dioxide, with its grassy, large open spaces and trees. It's quite popular with dog walkers, runners and picnickers. The garden is occasionally used for concerts, too.

The special gardens in the park include the Hedge Garden, Herb Garden, Rose Garden and the Shakespeare Garden.

Johannesburg Art Gallery

Located in Joubert Park, the Johannesburg Art Gallery is the largest on the subcontinent, and its collection is larger than Cape Town's Iziko South African National Art Gallery. It houses Dutch paintings from the 17th century, European art from the 18th and 19th century, and contemporary art from the 20th century, including international and local art.

Museum Africa

The Museum Africa includes pieces of all types of African material culture and cultural history. After apartheid's fall in 1994, the museum was renamed and refurbished. It holds collections of African culture from the entire continent, including collections of head-rests, tokens and musical instruments.

Gold Reef City

Gold Reef City is among the largest theme parks in Africa. Its theme is the 1800's gold rush that led to the city's establishment. It has some of Africa's fastest, tallest thrill rides, along with tame family rides and a 4D theater. It is one of the country's most popular amusement parks.

Montecasino

Montecasino is a casino and leisure complex in Johannesburg. It opened in November of 2000 and attracts more than nine million visitors a year. The design replicates a Tuscan village in ancient time. In addition to gaming in the casino, it also offers events and family entertainment.

Montecasino presents award-winning, world-class shows, from live concerts from well-known artists to popular comedies. They also present musicals and classic theater shows.

Lion & Safari Park

The new, larger Lion & Safari Park has moved away from what used to be a type of "petting zoo" to a more realistic safari experience. It's located in the Cradle of Humankind.

You can watch predators like wild dogs, lions and cheetah in custom habitats that represent their natural environment well. Predators are kept in complete separate areas from the buck and antelope, so you don't have to see any vicious hunting scenes play out.

Johannesburg Night-Life

Joburg doesn't slow down one step as it goes from daytime to nighttime. There are plenty of clubs, pubs and bars that will keep you dancing all through the night.

Hush

This glamorous club is classy, edgy and modern. You can live out your favorite dreams in their fantasy universe. They have some of the best DJs in South Africa. The club features lounges for relaxation and visual delights for your mind and eyes.

Icon Sandton

This club bills itself as the latest sophisticated and upmarket night club in Joburg. It's located in the center of Sandton, and their guests are a trendy and mature crowd. The decoration is tasteful and the classy atmosphere offers a chance to enjoy a great selection of music genres over the weekend nights.

The Sands

This is an open air commercial bar and club, located in Sandton. They play host to many events and parties, with top DJs. The busiest party nights are Friday and Saturday. They are open the other nights of the week, too.

7. Special Events in Johannesburg

Chinese New Year – end of January

Old Chinatown breaks into celebration in the streets on Chinese New Year. The festivities include dragon and lion performances, tai chi and kung fu displays and traditional singing, dancing and drumming. They even have extensive fireworks displays. They have lots of food in the street festival booths.

Johannesburg International Mozart Festival – January – February

The Mozart Festival of Johannesburg is held each year and boasts a week of cultural events and amazing concerts.

Joburg Fest Tap Craft Beer Festival – April

Check out more than 180 of South Africa's finest craft beers, wines, whiskeys, gins and ciders. Each sip is special, in this warm and friendly setting. It offers only the best of SA craft brewers, and is a worthwhile event to attend, whether you are into home brewing or just want to sample what the city has to offer.

Juliet Cullinan Standard Bank Wine Festival - May

This wine festival offers everyone something to savor. It's held every May, at the Summer Place of Hyde Park. Listen to talks by cellar-celebrities in the industry or just enjoy tasting the variety of wines, at the long-running festival that showcases the finest wineries on the Cape.

Youth Day – June

This public holiday was once called Soweto Day. It is held each year in remembrance of the 20,000 students in Soweto who, in 1976, began a brave protest march for equal civil liberties and rights.

Standard Bank Joy of Jazz – September

This is the largest annual jazz festival for Joburgers. It includes an emphasis on jazz but features other musical styles, too. It has hosted more than 200 international and local artists performing at various venues in the city.

Jozi Film Festival – September

This is the only multi-genre, independent film festival in Johannesburg. They show documentaries (long and short), short fiction films and feature films, from South Africa and international studious. They also feature student films.

Arts Alive – September through October

This vibrant festival starts in September each year and runs for 6-8 weeks. It highlights various aspects of the culture and history of South Africa through performance art and modern art. You can attend workshops, watch parades in the street, listen to musical performances and attend other activities.

AfroPunk Fest – December

For the purposes of this festival, "afro" means having been born in Africa, with its inherent heritage and spirit. The "punk" aspect means rebels who look to the future with curiosity and simplicity. When you put them together, AfroPunk defines culture by the creative, collective actions of groups and individuals alike. It's a safe festival, a blank space where you can "freak out", and live your life the way you would like to, while trying to make sense of the broader canvas of the world.

8.Safety in Johannesburg

High crime once made South Africa a dangerous place to visit, but most crime today occurs in the poorest townships, which you will not frequent as a tourist. Taking sensible precautions, you can thoroughly enjoy your trip to Johannesburg.

Road Safety

Johannesburg is famous for carjackers, but the incidence rate is relatively low. You'll probably be taking transit or taxis rather than renting a car, anyway. The roads are confusing and traffic is heavy. Whether you're driving or walking to a nearby attraction, watch out for the "taxi" minibuses. The drivers often speed.

Robbery

Even after apartheid, the disparity between the wealthy and the poor in South Africa is huge. The rich and poor cohabitate here, and it's natural that some problems occur for this reason.

When you're out in public, don't wear flashy jewelry or watches. Don't get your camera out unless you're ready to use it. Choose a hotel with 24-hour security. If you use an ATM, choose one in a busy area, during daylight hours.

Women's Safety

South Africa has rape and sexual assault statistics that could scare you if you didn't know that the perpetrators do not usually target tourists. That doesn't mean caution should be forgotten. If you travel outside the city, stay in groups whenever possible.

9. Conclusion

Johannesburg doesn't have any snow-capped mountains or lush beaches. For these reasons and others, tourists often overlook the city. However, it is a cultural center with many types of entertainment that run day and night. It is also the location where apartheid fell, and there are many museums and memorials to this historic event.

The human race also evolved in the area around Johannesburg, and this is another interesting reason to visit. The city holds a brilliant blend of modern life and traditional heritage. Many of the top African institutes of the arts are in this city.

The people in Johannesburg are simple, and have a joyous lifestyle and great tastes in music. The city is surrounded by tropical rainforests and other examples of natural beauty. The foods served are a unique mixture of indigenous and Asian foods. The weather conditions are conducive to a pleasing vacation, too.

Made in the USA
Columbia, SC
15 April 2022